MARTI
A LIFE INSPIRED

MW01256590

Introduction

Martin Luther is arguably one of the most influential people in the past millennium. He is perhaps most notably recognized for nailing the "Ninety-five Theses" to the door of the Wittenberg Castle church, effectively initiating what is now Christian Protestantism. Luther was radical, wittily sarcastic, and rebellious against the traditional establishments of the Church. Whatever Luther could do to progress and defend Scripture, he did, even at the risk of his life. He is often referred to as the "Great Reformer" and the father of Lutheranism. His devotion and passion for the word of God would become his driving force. He would face ridicule, opposition, and at times, daily death-threats, yet his grasp on the word of God would ultimately preserve him for a lifetime of far-reaching accomplishment.

Among the best ways to understand the tenor of Luther is with a firsthand account of his writings. His boldness leaps from the page: "Let us not lose the Bible, but with diligence, in fear and invocation of God, read and preach it." He viewed himself as not providing a radically new interpretation of Scripture, but a more innocent, stripped-down version, void of the interpretive manipulation he believed was being committed by the Roman Catholic Church. Luther believed Scripture was intended for everyone who had an ear for God's word, and not just priests, whose role was to deliver it to the people. This view of Scripture would become his so-called anthem of life. With diligence and in holy fear of God, he would go on to defend all of Scripture against the corruptions of the Church, while asserting, "my conscience is captive to the word of God."

Famous for speaking against the abuses of the church, Luther declared, "If anyone despises my fraternal warning, I am free from his blood in the last judgment. It is better that I should die a thousand times than retract one syllable of the condemned articles. And as they excommunicated me for the sacrilege of heresy, so I excommunicated them in the name of the sacred truth of God. Christ will judge whose excommunication will stand. Amen."

How would Luther come to such a place of boldness, courage, and resolve? In hindsight, one can see how God crafted Luther from his childhood to adulthood to be used as a high instrument in preserving the truths of Scripture. And it is through the workings of his life that he would begin to find his path—a path that would not only impact his life, but those lives in the generations to come.

Above all, understanding Martin Luther involves more than just learning about the great epithets attached to his name; it is to understand, as Martin Marty notes, that Luther was a "wrestler with God" and a "God-obsessed seeker of certainty and assurance" in a time of social, political, and personal unrest. Yes, he fought for the truths of Scripture. Yes, he had enough courage to allow his pursuit and understanding of God to impact the world around him. But ironically, if, during his time, there were no corruption of the Church, there would be no Martin Luther, and there would be no Great Reformation. Perhaps someone else would have come along. We do not know. But it is interesting to consider the kind of faith and religion we might have today if it weren't for Luther and his followers, who aimed to preserve the truths of Scripture.

Background and Birth:

Luther was born in Eisleben, Germany, on November 10, 1483 to Hans and Margarethe Lindemann Luder. His mother was a hardworking woman who raised three children, while his father became a successful leaseholder of mines. Luther saw his parents in a slightly different, not-so-positive light, however. In his own words, Luther wrote, "I am a peasant's son. My father, grandfather, and great-grandfather were genuine peasants. My father was a miner and my mother carried wood from the forest on her back; they both worked the flesh off their bones in order to bring up their children." Whatever the case may be, Luther no doubt had a great appreciation for the type of work ethic his parents displayed.

However, many of Luther's childhood memories recall just how harsh and strict both his parents were. Of his mother's discipline, he wrote that on one occasion, "for the sake of stealing a nut, [his] mother once beat [him] until the blood flowed." Luther's father was no different in the way he disciplined his son. Luther wrote, "my father once whipped me so hard, I ran away. I hated him until he finally managed to win me back." But interestingly enough, although the discipline he received was harsh and would be considered abusive today, Luther wrote that he knew his parents meant it for his own good. Indeed, Luther credits his life of discipline to his childhood experiences. Hard work and perseverance were consistent themes throughout his immensely productive life.

Yet, with each "lesson" he gleaned from his parents, the harsh discipline he incurred also began shaping his initial view of God. Early on, Luther viewed God as a cruel and strict judge, someone he endlessly had to try to please for fear of bringing judgment and condemnation upon himself. Throughout much of his young adult life, Luther struggled tremendously with his view of God, and view that took years to resolve.

It helps to understand Luther's inner struggle with God-as-wrathful-judge by considering his surroundings. This particular view of God prevailed and was perpetuated by the Holy Roman Empire's social and religious views at that time. Luther grew up straddling two vastly opposing historical epochs: medieval and modern. In fact, historians frequently argue that Luther himself was among the biggest driving factors in the transformation. The medieval period was defined by religious and social oppression, where individuals were controlled by their local governments, which in turn where controlled by the larger kingdom in conjunction with the Roman Catholic Church. At the same time, Indivualism was becoming a more popular way to see oneself in the world. People wanted to experience the world for themselves. Out of the medieval period grew increasing dissatisfaction with obedience and a growing regard for one's conscience. In their social and political commitment to medieval oppression, citizens of Europe were experiencing the beginnings of a Renaissance.

In that time, plagues reduced Europe's total population by 30–60 percent. Miners, like Luther's father, were particularly susceptible to infection. Physical illness was often attributed to spiritual causes, so the common practice was for miners to baptize their children, believing that the baptism would drive out demonic forces. So it was for Luther. His parents baptized him the day after his birth, on November 11, which happened to be a day reserved for commemorating St. Martin, who lived in the 400s. Luther's parents, seeing the spiritual connection of their son's baptism with the saint, decided to name their son Martin. Such an act was thought to have been performed to please God, hoping to gain His grace, and to set their son on a path of salvation. Because of his family's beliefs, and the common practices of Europe during that period, Luther inherited a God-fearing mentality.

Early on, his father had a grand desire for Luther to become a lawyer, and Luther initially strove to meet his father's expectations. Growing up, he was socio-economically privileged and was therefore able to receive a first-rate education. He went on to Latin school and studied the classical languages while also being trained in the doctrines and practices of the church. He eventually obtained his bachelor's degree in liberal arts, followed by a master's degree in grammar, logic, rhetoric, and metaphysics— preparing himself well for a career in the law.

Luther's Road to Damascus:

In the book of Acts, the apostle Paul had an encounter with the living God on the road to Damascus that forever changed his life. As he was en route to persecute Christians, Paul was blinded by a light that stopped him dead in his tracks. Then a voice said, "Why are you persecuting me?" After Paul questioned where the voice was coming from, he was answered with the words, "I am Jesus of Nazareth, whom you are persecuting." Paul's journey was momentous for the history of Christianity, as it provided him with a revelation as to his religious mission. It allowed him to see that Jesus Christ was delivering the gospel, and Paul was to follow suit as a disciple.

Luther's "Road to Damascus" presented itself a little differently, but it was no less impactful.

In 1505, Luther found himself caught in a storm. As the storm thundered, it appeared that the heavens were crying out to him. He became so terrified at that moment, he feared he would likely die. He thus cried out, "Help, dear Saint Anne!" who was the mother of Mary. In that moment, he made a promise to himself and to God that if his life were spared, he would become a monk, devoting himself fully to the purposes of God. Luther wrote, "I entered the spiritual state for no other reason than to serve God and to please Him in eternity." Luther identified in that moment God's ultimate power for grace. Luther believed that he was spared from the storm because of God's grace, and that belief began to shape Luther's larger picture of God, God's purpose, and our relationship to Him. Most historians recognize this not as a "transformational moment" so much as a "tipping point". Luther's choice to become a monk was probably a long time coming, despite officially aiming at a career in law for the sake of his father's wishes.

Still, from that moment on, at the age of twenty-two, Luther decided that he was called to become a monk. In those days, it was generally believed that if you didn't pursue life as a monk or priest, you were somehow a second-class citizen. Of course, today it is accepted that one can glorify God in whatever one does. But in those times, seeking to live a life "pleasing" to God almost always translated to entering the monastery.

But regardless of his father's demands and desires, Martin Luther pursued a life that he believed would greatly honor and serve God. For him, it became so clear that God was calling him to the monastery, he could do nothing other than follow the call. He prayed that God would find him worthy enough to continuing in devotion:

> Lord Jesus Christ, who didst deign to clothe thyself in our mortality, we beseech thee out of thine immeasurable goodness to bless the habit which the holy fathers have chosen as a sign of innocence and renunciation. May this thy servant, Martin Luther, who

takes the habit, be also clothed in thine immortality, O thou who livest and reignest with God the Father and the Holy Ghost, God from eternity to eternity, Amen.

Luther, the German Monk

By today's standards, Luther may be diagnosed with manic-depressive disorder. He could have heightened moods, which included periods of extreme depression. It's no question that many factors contributed to his mental health. He expressed much despair in his early years, as he was always under the impression that God would judge him with wrath and fire. And to make matters worse, he was struggling not only with a God he couldn't seem to please, but also with a father he disappointed by his move from law to religion. One can imagine Luther's inner turmoil. But Luther learned to channel his inner struggles—which might normally have been seen as a source of weakness or deficiency—to help further his pursuit of God

As Luther entered into the monastic life, his chief pursuit was pure: he wanted to make peace with God. He did everything in his power to pursue faith and religion practice to the highest degree. Early on, he would try to perfect the monastic religious exercises, especially prayer. Luther often prayed seven times a day in a strictly regimented schedule. It is recorded that monks, after eight hours of sleep, were awakened by a bell past midnight. They would then signal the sign of a cross and pull on their robes. As the bell rang a second time, they would sprinkle themselves with holy water and kneel in prayer to God. Each period of prayer would then end with what is called the *Salve Regina*: "Save, O Queen, Thou Mother of mercy, our life, our delight and our hope. To Thee, we exiled sons of Eve lift up our cry. To Thee, we sigh as we languish in this vale of tears. Be Thou our advocate, Sweet Virgin Mary, pray for us. Thou holy Mother of God."

But later, Luther realized that his early days as a monk were driven out of a motivation of fear, not love. As he spent time in prayer, he held in his mind an image of God as a strict judge who required perfect obedience. So often, in Luther's early writings, he communicated this tremendous fear that he was unworthy merely to pray and stand before a holy and righteous God. He wrote, "I am dust and ashes and full of sin." As a result, Luther tried to keep to the strictest of disciplines when it came to the study of God's word, prayer, and the practice of sacraments.

Specifically, through his early pursuits of perfecting the religious exercises of prayer, he became so aware of his sinfulness that it caused intense inner conflict and despair. Here is where his depressive nature was perpetuated by this constant fear of a vengeful God. Luther confessed even the "smallest" of sins so often to the priest that the priest became tired of Luther. Although other monks said that Luther was exceptional because of his strict discipline to prayer and fasting, for Luther it was never enough. He would look at God's commands of perfection and wonder how it was possible to achieve them, for even his acts of obedience were tainted with sinful motivations.

This pursuit drove Luther to great despair and agony, even as he was honored early on by being selected to perform mass. Luther believed in the church doctrine that Jesus was literally present in human form through the sacraments of the bread and the wine. Given his inner turmoil, Luther wondered how a sinful young priest could present the sacraments when a holy God would be present. He reflected:

> I was utterly stupefied and terror-stricken. I thought to myself, "With what tongues what shall I address such Majesty, seeing that all men ought to tremble in the presence of even an earthly prince? Who am I, that I should lift up mine eyes or raise my hands to the divine Majesty? The angels surround him. At his nod the earth trembles. And shall I, a miserable little pygmy says, 'I want this, I ask for that?'"

What worried Luther even more was that his father would join his son in his first mass. It would be the first time he would talk to his father since leaving law school and entering the monastery. It's recorded that Luther had a discussion with his dad after the mass and asked, "Why are you so contrary to me becoming a monk?" Although Luther was officially an adult, one can picture Luther seeking the approval of his father as if he were still a young child.

While his father attempted to make amends by showing up to his mass and giving him a gift, he was still not ready to have a peaceful discussion about it. He responded by condemning Luther: "Have you never read the Bible that you should honor your father and mother? And here you have left your dear mother and me to look for ourselves in our old age."

Perhaps Luther expected a different response, as opposed to being made to feel guilty. Luther, although fully aware of God's command to honor his father and mother, was also fully aware that the gospel called him to forsake his family. But Luther's father questioned whether Luther was genuinely following after God or simply following Satan in the guise of an angel.

This thought affected Luther considerably. He was again haunted, and he entered into a depressive state. Was his experience of the thunderstorm truly a detour sent by God? Or was he following after the deceptive plans of Satan? Again, Luther was confronted by the thought that he was a disappointment and failure to both God and his father. As time past, it would become apparent to Luther that, throughout the years, his experience had been, in fact, one given by God.

In 1507, at the young age of twenty-four, Luther became an ordained priest. Then, after being recommended by other priests and monks to pursue further studies, he continued on to finish his doctoral degree five years later, making the promise to defend all of Scripture as a minister and teacher.

Most pivotal in his studies was coming into contact with humanist ideas, specifically the mantra *ad fontes*, translated as "back to the source." After earning his doctoral degree, he was admitted as a theology professor at the University of Wittenberg, where he would do just that: go back to the source of Scripture, teaching directly from Psalms, Romans, Galatians, and Hebrews, over the span of six years. As Luther studied the Bible in its original languages of Hebrew (Old Testament) and Greek (New Testament), he began grappling with the core truths of Scripture. Most pivotal in Luther's transformation of his faith was his preparation for and teaching of his lectures on the book of Romans. Luther would thus experience another "thunderstorm," but this time within the very chambers of his heart.

Tower at Wittenberg

One of the most influential moments of Luther's life occurred within a tower at Wittenberg in which he taught. He began reading the book of Romans when he came across the words written by the Apostle Paul, "the just shall live by faith." A deep conviction pierced his heart. He realized that throughout all his years living in the monastery and all his years studying, he had never been taught that salvation was a result of faith as opposed to works. The problem for Luther lay in having a lack of understanding of both the Old Testament and New Testament. He wrote:

> [B]esides the law (in the OT), there are certain promises and sentences of grace ... the New Testament then is a book wherein is written the Gospel of God's promises, and the acts of those that believed, and those that believed not ... the proper and chief doctrine of the New Testament is grace and peace through the forgiveness of sins declared in Christ, so the proper and

chief doctrine of the Old Testament is, through the law, to discover sin and to required good works and obedience.

Though Luther had sought other priests to help assuage his inner conflict about his inability to meet the standards of God, no one taught what he was reading now in the book of Romans. He wondered why no priest had explained what Apostle Paul taught.

Luther realized that sin wasn't necessarily a list of offenses he had committed against God, but rather that the very nature of man was corrupt. So, no matter how many sins he confessed or how often he tried to receive some penance, it would never address the core issue: he was in need of sincere forgiveness from a holy God.

As he continued to wrestle with these truths, he began to realize the lack of biblical preaching from the priests and how they emphasized the necessity of works rather than faith. This gravely concerned Luther. He came to see the tremendous chasm that existed between the priest and the congregant. The congregant had to depend on the priest for the interpretation of Scripture because the laity was simply unable to read Latin, a privilege of the priestly and wealthy classes. Whereas today there are a multitude of Bibles with different translations in different languages, Luther grew up in a time where he didn't have this luxury. As a result, the priest had all the religious authority; without the priest, there would be no understanding of the Bible.

As he reflected on the truths of Scripture (namely the book of Romans and the doctrine of justification), he began to challenge the traditional teachings of the church. This would only propel him to learn to expound Scripture himself and seek truth as the Bible taught, as opposed to relying on what

the other priests taught. As he did so, it only highlighted the

truth that the church was abusing its authority.

Indulgences

In 1510, Luther traveled to Rome to appeal to the pope. It would take him three months to travel from Germany to Rome, crossing over mountainous terrain that ominously foreshadowed the many obstacles he would face as he confronted the pope and the establishment of the church.

Upon arriving in Rome, Luther was taken aback by its magnificence. Aesthetically, he was moved by the vast buildings and the craftsmanship of the architecture. He found much beauty in Rome, and he expected that the monks and leaders of the church lived a spiritually beautiful lifestyle accordingly. To Luther's shock, he found out that the opposite was true. He witnessed first-hand that monks in Rome lived wicked and sinful lifestyles that were antithetical to the teachings of Scripture.

One day, as Luther was walking up the steps of the Scala Santa in Rome, the same steps people believed could free the soul,

Paul's words from the book of Romans, "the just shall live by faith," arrested Luther once more. And immediately he turned and walked down the steps, a significant moment for Luther. As opposed to following the tradition of climbing all the steps, by stepping away from the ritual, he began to put into practice the words in Scripture regarding justification by challenging the notion of salvation through his works.

The year 1512 proved pivotal in the formation of Luther's faith. He worked full-time as a professor and began teaching for the next six years on books of the Bible that would become his foundation for faith: Psalms, Romans, Galatians, and Hebrews. Collectively, his studies on these particular books would gird his understanding of the gospel as presented in Scripture. As opposed to hearing the lessons of Scripture as told by other monks or church authorities, his personal studies helped him begin to question what others taught.

As God was beginning to form Luther's identity within the gospel, Luther became even more aware of the corruptions of the church, notably the sale of indulgences—the means by which church priests would convince people that the church could purchase the forgiveness of sins. For Luther, not only was the sale of indulgences in direct opposition to what Scripture taught, but it also encouraged people to live a life of sin. And while the people who bought indulgences were guilty of sin, for Luther, the church and its priests were taking full advantage of their power and position of heralding God's word and so held the greater portion of blame.

Also, as a priest, Luther started realizing that people weren't coming to him for confession as often as they should. Instead, they were traveling to different cities that sold indulgences. Indulgences were sold by the church and allowed people to "buy their salvation" and thereby "atone for their sins."

Different priests and monks sold these indulgences, some more successfully than others. Johann Tezel was one such monk who sold indulgences. His particularly famous marketing spiel for selling indulgences went something like this: "When the money clangs in the box, the soul springs up to heaven." He and others would also teach that indulgences could be bought for loved ones who already passed. Indulgences would then provide "favor and grace" if the person had not lived a God-fearing life on earth.

Such behavior outraged Luther, who later asserted that greed was the motivating factor for the sale of indulgences and that neither the pope nor the church had any authority to forgive anyone's sin based on the sale of indulgences. After experiencing firsthand the Roman Catholic Church's hypocrisy, it became the ultimate source of Luther's contention.

Luther decided to approach the abuse of Scripture through the sale of indulgences by debating the issue among other theologians. At this time, the common practice to call for a debate was to post a list of propositions—or theses— to defend on the door of the Castle Church. Such posting would initiate the debate. This was the general context surrounding Luther's famous posting of his 95 Theses. It wasn't just blatant disregard for the church but a challenge, albeit an intellectual one. To his credit, Luther's actions weren't entirely customary. His public defense of Scriptures and its truths came steeped in bitter condemnation of the Church and its followers. His Ninety-five Theses ignited rebellion and provoked intense discussion regarding the malpractices of the pope and the church. The document famously paved the way for the (still ongoing) Protestant Reformation.

Interestingly enough, Luther never intended for the Ninety-five Theses to reach so many people. In fact, the theses were translated and distributed without his permission. And Luther certainly never intended to bring reformation to the church as a whole. Although he was against the practices of the church, Luther was more comfortable seeking reform in the arena of theological education. He once wrote to his friend regarding his lack of impulse to protest against the church:

> I could use two secretaries. I do almost nothing during the day but write letters. I am a conventional preacher, reader at meals, parochial preacher, director of studies, overseer of eleven monasteries, superintendent of the fish pond at Litzkau, referee of the squabble at Torgau, lecturer on Paul, collector of material for a commentary on the Psalms, and then, as I said, I am overwhelmed with letters. I rarely have full time for the canonical hours and for saying mass, not to mention my own temptations with the world, the flesh, and the Devil. You see how lazy I am.

To be sure, Luther wasn't lazy; he had much on his plate. But amidst the self-deprecating sarcasm and humor, and his initial plans to remain in theological studies, it was clear that God had bigger plans.

Transformation

More revolutionary for Luther than the posting of his ninety-five theses was his own transformation that year. Luther continued to live his life as a priest and monk. Although he pursued perfection in his obedience toward Christ, he was still convinced that he was a sinner under the hands of a strict divine authority. This conviction fostered inner turmoil for Luther because he found righteousness to be something unattainable and unreachable in his own pursuits. He wrote, "I hated a righteous God punishing sinners. I rebelled against God. My conscience was wounded. I gnashed inwardly and yet ever came back to the verse that the righteousness of God is revealed in the Gospel."

But what Luther now began to hate would be the very truth to set him free and transform his life. The words of Paul in Romans 1:17 convicted him again: "For therein is the righteousness of God revealed from faith to faith: as it is written, the just shall live by faith." From that momentous occasion at a tower in Wittenberg when he was first convicted by the words of Paul, to the moment after he posted his Ninety-five Theses, these words began to take form within his soul. Luther wrote:

> At least thinking over the matter for days and nights, God showed me mercy and the connection of these words with the following sentence that the "just shall live by faith." I saw the meaning of the verse to be: "Through the Gospel is revealed that righteousness of God by which the merciful God declares the believers righteous."

There began a shift in Luther's view of God, a change from a wrathful and harsh judge to a merciful and loving Father. He continued, "Now I felt myself new-born and in Paradise. All the Holy Scriptures looked different to me. This passage in Paul appeared to me as the gate of Paradise." For Luther, salvation was now made possible by the gift of God by sending Jesus Christ to die for the atonement of his sins. No longer was he pressured and bound with the constant worries of trying to please God out of fear that he would be eternally damned. He finally was able to rest in the gospel truth laid out in Romans by the Apostle Paul: one is justified and made righteous by faith in Christ.

Luther wrote,

> But a true Christian says, "I believe in Jesus Christ my Lord and Savior," who gave Himself for my sins, and is at God's right hand, and intercedes for me; fall I into sin, as, alas! Oftentimes I do, I am sorry for it. I rise again and am an enemy of sin. So that we plainly see, the true Christian faith is far different from the faith and religion of the pope. But human strength and nature are not able to accomplish this true Christian

faith without the Holy Spirit. It can do no more than take refuge in its own deserts.

These are words that shifted Luther from monk to reformer. Whereas he would have beat himself over for his sins by pursuing obedience, he could now rest in the perfect work of Jesus. He was transformed by the Holy Spirit through the word of Scripture.

He never stopped pursuing obedience. The profound difference lay in his object of salvation. In the past, Luther had fundamentally depended on his own good works for salvation. Now, Luther's purpose of salvation lay in the finished work of Jesus as He died for the sins of the world (including Luther's) and rose again from the dead. With Jesus being the root of his salvation, Luther would continue to pursue obedience as an effort of devotion.

Three Treatises

Luther's provocative stance against the church expressed in his Ninety-five Theses brought him notoriety. In 1519, he debated a prominent theologian named John Eck. Within that debate, Luther sharpened his view of authority and where it lay. Was power to reside in a priest or the church? Luther publicly defended the truth that the Bible alone was the basis for truth.

Although Luther faced threats on his life, and was imprisoned and persecuted, he nonetheless said, "Whatever I do, I wish to not do according to man's pleasure, but according to God's will. If the work be not begun in His name, it will soon come to pass; if it is begun in His name, let Him have His own way." Luther possessed confidence, courage, and an unyielding passion for defending the truth of Scripture against the corrupt practices of the church.

He published several writings that would further spread his defense of scriptural authority. The first treatise Luther wrote was the *Address to the German Nobility*. As Luther began to realize the impact of his writings and public defenses , he feared that chaos would ensue within the church of believers. He feared that believers would respond to the church and its corruptions with vengeful anger, so in his first treatise, he wrote to German princes to call a special counsel to put a hold on the pope's authority. Luther used strong language directed against the pope and the church. He wrote:

> The popes have built three strong walls which are obstacles to any true Reformation. In the first place, if you mention temporal power, they claim temporal power has no authority over them, since spiritual power I higher than temporal power. Secondly, if you refer to the Scriptures, they answer that no one can by right interpret the Scriptures save the pope; and in the

third instance, if you mention a General Council they feign that the pope has the sole right to call a General Council. Now may God help us and give us one of the trumpets with which the walls of Jericho were overthrown, so that we can blow down these walls of straw and paper.

The second treatise was the *Babylonian Captivity of the Church*. In this writing, Luther deployed heavy theological truth in defense of Scripture, and in doing so, he condemned the practices of the church. He argued three main errors within the church: the Lord's Supper, transubstantiation, and the Eucharistic ceremony.

Luther argued that the Lord's Supper should model Christ's words given to the disciples during the Passover in Luke 22:14–23. Jesus instituted the Lord's Supper as including both the bread and the wine, as opposed to what the Church was practicing—the bread alone. The second doctrine Luther addressed was transubstantiation, which condemned the view of the Church that only the essence of Christ would be present as the bread was taken during the Lord's Supper. Luther argued for transubstantiation, which stated that Jesus was not only there in essence, but also literally embodied in the bread. (This doctrine would ultimately be a point of conflict within the Protestant Reformation.)

The third doctrine Luther mentioned would drive home Luther's whole argument regarding the practices of the church. It was common during the Lord's Supper for only an ordained priest to administer the sacraments. Luther argued that there should not be a "special" order for ordained priests, but rather that through Christ's sacrifice, all believers were made priests. Therefore, all believers had access to God through Christ.

Luther's third treatise become one of his most influential and well-known pieces of writing, *On the Liberty of the Christian Man*. In his original address, he appealed to the pope (Leo X). Luther was aware that he was not just fighting a man in power but a whole system entrenched within the traditions of the church. But by addressing the pope as the Antichrist, Luther accomplished two objectives: condemning the practices of the pope personally and those of the church as a whole. He wrote provocatively in his introduction:

> Most blessed father, in all the controversies of the past three years I have ever been mindful of you, and although your adulterers have driven me to appeal to a council in defiance of the futile decrees of your predecessors, I have never suffered myself because of their stupid tyranny to hold your Beatitude in despite. To be sure, I have spoken sharply against impious doctrine, but did not Christ call his adversaries a

generation of vipers, blind guides, and hypocrites? And did not Paul refer to his opponents as dogs, concision, and sons of the Devil? Who could have been more biting than the prophets? I contend with no one about his life, but only concerning the Word of Truth. I look upon you less as Leo the Lion than as Daniel in the lion's den of Babylon. You may have three or four learned and excellent cardinals, but what are they among so many? The Roman curia deserves not you but Satan himself. What under heaven is more pestilence I am inveighing against your person? Beware of the sirens who would make you not simply a man but half a god. You are a servant of servants. Do not listen to those who say that none can be Christians without your authority, who make you the lord of heaven, hell, and purgatory.

Luther was intentionally crossing a line by addressing the pope as the Antichrist. Not only was he attacking an individual who was the leader and authority of the church, but he was also attacking the whole of the church establishment. Despite this knowledge, however, Luther remained bold in his efforts to defend Scripture.

This treatise was particularly instrumental in undermining the misplaced authority of the pope. When the pope and priests contended that they had manifest authority over all believers, Luther referred to Scripture in asserting the priesthood of all believers. He invoked Scripture in his introduction:

> "For though I am free from all men, I have made myself a slave to all," (1 Corinthians 9:19) and "owe no one anything, except to love one another" (Romans 13:8). Love by its very nature is ready to serve and be subject

to him who is loved. So Christ, although He was Lord of all, was "born of woman, born under the law" (Galatians 4:4), and therefore was at the same time a free man and servant, "in the form of God" and "of a servant" (Philippians 2:6–7).

Luther thus argued that all believers held the same position before God because of Christ's gift of salvation. No pope or priest should be considered separate, because they were no different from other men in nature.

These three treatises profoundly influenced all of Europe. They formed the initial substance behind the Reformation of the church, and they influenced a multitude of theologians, most notably John Calvin (1509–1564).

Challenging the Establishment

As Luther continued to defend the authority of Scripture, his attacks on the church—and specifically on practices related to indulgences—grew more vigorous. While many others may have had similar thoughts as Luther regarding the corruption of the church, no one else had demonstrated the ability or courage to articulate his position against the church in such an effective, public way. Soon, Luther's words would catch fire and spread all across the continent. Nations split over Luther's teachings and the practices of the church. While many agreed with Luther, others questioned whether Luther's words were an accurate representation of Scripture.

The Roman Church came under attack as Luther's ideas gained momentum. Pope Leo X had a supreme hatred for Luther and tried a multitude of methods to try to discredit Luther and put an end to his attacks. He referred to Luther as a "drunken German" and sought to arrest him. Ultimately, the pope issued a papal bull that denounced everything Luther taught as being "contrary to all love and reverence for the Holy Roman Church" and laid the grounds for Luther's excommunication from the Church. The papal bull contained a total of forty-one propositions condemning Luther and his statements. Pope Leo X, in noted excerpts of the bull, declared:

> With the advice and consent of these our venerable brothers, with mature deliberation on each and every one of the above theses, and by the authority of Almighty God, the blessed Apostles Peter and Paul, and our own authority, we condemn, reprobate, and reject completely each of these theses or errors as either heretical, scandalous, false, offensive to pious ears or seductive of simple minds, and against Catholic truth. We likewise condemn, reprobate, and reject completely the books and all the writings and sermons of the said Martin, whether in Latin or any other language, containing the said errors or any one of them; and we

wish them to be regarded as utterly condemned, reprobated, and rejected. We forbid each and every one of the faithful of either sex, in virtue of holy obedience and under the above penalties to be incurred automatically, to read, assert, preach, praise, print, publish, or defend them. Indeed, immediately after the publication of this letter these works, wherever they may be, shall be sought out carefully by the ordinaries and others [ecclesiastics and regulars], and under each and every one of the above penalties shall be burned publicly and solemnly in the presence of the clerics and people.

Although Luther's writings were publicly burned in some regions, nothing could prevent the fire that was already ablaze within Luther. He responded directly to Pope Leo X's papal bull, saying, "I exhort and admonish you in the Lord to repent and make an end of these diabolical blasphemies. I regard your bishopric as possessed by Satan and as the accursed abode of the Antichrist, whom we not only cannot obey but must detest and execrate as the chief enemy of Christ."

Not only did Luther make his thoughts known to the pope, but he also burned the papal bull and all of its forty-one propositions, alongside the entire law of the church. He wrote a letter called the *Assertion of All the Articles Wrongly Condemned in the Roman Bull*, which aimed to directly refute the propositions laid out by the pope.

Actions like these, are part of what made Luther such a dynamic figure and leader— he perfectly demonstrated the radical nature of his thought. Not only did he possess the training and intellect to argue with the most notable theologians, but he also possessed boldness and courage to stand up against the established traditions of the Church.

"Here I Stand"

Eventually, in 1521, charges were brought against Luther before Emperor Charles V at the Diet of Worms. There, alongside the most powerful and influential leaders of the Reformation movement, he was given an opportunity to remain a free man and within the church. It is recorded that nearly two thousand people turned out to the hearing to witness how Luther responded to the claims and condemnation against the church.

Luther was certainly bold and sarcastically honest in his writing, we hear the resolve that Luther maintained amidst the death sentence that could be placed before him. He wrote:

> You ask me what I shall do if I am called by the emperor. I will go even if I am too sick to stand on my feet. If Caesar calls me, God calls me. If violence is used, as well it may be, I commend my cause to God. He lives and reigns who saved the three youths from the fiery

furnace of the king of Babylon, and if He will not save
me, my head is worth nothing compared with Christ.
This is no time to think of safety. I must take care that
the gospel is not brought into contempt by our fear to
confess and seal our teaching with our blood.

Elsewhere he wrote to one of his friends:

This is not the time to cringe, but to cry aloud when our
Lord Jesus Christ is damned, reviled and blasphemed. If
you exhort me to humility, I exhort you to pride. The
matter is very serious. We see Christ suffer. If hitherto
we ought to have been silent and humble, I ask you
whether now, when the blessed Savior is mocked, we
should not fight for him. My father, the danger is
greater than many think. Now applies the word of the
gospel, "He who confesses me before men, him will I
confess in the presence of my father, and he who denies

me before men, him will I deny." I write this candidly to you because I am afraid you hesitate between Christ and the pope, though they are diametrically contrary. Let us pray that the Lord Jesus will destroy the son of perdition with the breath of his mouth ... I burned the pope's books at first with fear and trembling, but now I am lighter in heart than I have ever been in my life.

What great insight these passages offer into the character and spiritual growth of Luther. An overview of his life paints the picture of an emboldened man. In this portrait, however, we see that Luther, too, was a man like any other who had his reservations and fears. Yet with every step of obedience, according to the convictions of Scripture, Luther grew in courage and confidence. As he stood before the emperor and authorities, he was prepared to die for the gospel.

Luther was ordered to take back all of the statements he had made against the church, to which he responded, "Should I recant at this point, I would open the door to more tyranny and impiety and it will be all the worse should it appear that I had done so at the instance of the Holy Roman Empire." And as listeners were caught up in his great crescendo of words, Luther proclaimed, "Unless I am refuted and convicted by testimonies of the Scriptures, I am conquered by the Holy Scriptures I have quoted and my conscience is captive to the Word of God." Most famously, Luther would speak in German, *"Hier stehe ich. Ich kann nicht anders. Gott helfe mir. Amen."* *(Here I stand; I cannot do otherwise. God help me. Amen.)*

A Mighty Fortress Is Our God

Many may not know that besides Luther's writings, he was also a hymn writer. It was during these challenging times, while defending Scripture, that he wrote a hymn still sung in today's churches, "A Mighty Fortress Is Our God."

A mighty fortress is our God, a bulwark never failing;
Our helper He, amid the flood of mortal ills prevailing:
For still our ancient foe doth seek to work us woe;
His craft and power are great, and, armed with cruel hate,
On earth is not his equal.
Did we in our own strength confide, our striving would be losing,
Were not the right Man on our side, the Man of God's own choosing:
Dost ask who that may be? Christ Jesus, it is He;
Lord Sabbath, His Name, from age to age the same,
And He must win the battle.

And though this world, with devils filled, should

threaten to undo us,

We will not fear, for God hath willed His truth to

triumph through us;

The Prince of Darkness grim, we tremble not for him;

His rage we can endure, for lo, his doom is sure,

One little word shall fell him.

That word above all earthly powers, no thanks to them,

abideth;

The Spirit and the gifts are ours through Him Who with

us sideth;

Let goods and kindred go, this mortal life also;

The body they may kill: God's truth abideth still,

His kingdom is forever.

How true these words were for Luther himself! One may ask
how Luther dared to stand up to the most influential and
powerful leaders of his day, risking his own life for the truth of

Scripture. The answer, for Luther, was clear enough: God was His mighty fortress, in whom he could place all his life.

Excommunicated

In response to Luther's bold address to the pope and the emperor, Luther was excommunicated, and his life was under constant threat by Church followers. There was nonetheless notable significance to this. Many of Luther's contemporaries considered his trial before the Emperor as mirroring the passion of Christ. Just as Jesus willingly accepted his fate to be martyred for the sins of humanity, so too Luther was willing to accept his sentence, sacrificing himself in order to defend the truth of Scripture.

Luther initially found no reason to hide, as he accepted his life as a martyr in the name of Christ. However, his supporters encouraged him to seek refuge, eventually escorting him on horseback to Wartburg Castle. There he would spend about three months accomplishing arguably his most important work, the translation of the entire New Testament from Greek into German.

But Luther's achievement came with a hefty price: he suffered from extreme melancholy from loneliness. Although he had the company of the warden and two boys who served him, no one could really empathize with all of Luther's struggles. He wrote, "I had rather burn on live coals than rot here." As Luther's active nature was stifled by living in hiding, one can sense in his writings the frustration and loneliness that he suffered alongside his physical distresses.

He wrote in 1527, "For more than a week, I was close to the gates of death and hell. I trembled in all my members. Christ was wholly lost. I was shaken by desperation and blasphemy of God."

At a time when mental health wasn't acknowledged and understood the way it is today, Luther struggled a great deal, not necessarily to find out the cause of his depression, but rather to find a solution to overcoming it. He had two main ways of confronting his depression: 1) He tried to tackle it directly, as a spiritual attack from Satan. Thus, he used episodes of depression as opportunities to seek the presence of God and proclaim God's word to his soul. 2) Luther sought to flee from his depressive episodes by redirecting his thoughts and being in the company of friends.

In these ways, Luther fought a lifelong battle against depression that he never fully overcame. He wrote, "When I go to bed, the Devil is always waiting for me." But above all, he always looked toward Christ in hope. During one of his most profound bouts with depression, Luther penned these lines of a hymn:

> A mighty bulwark is our God
>
> A doughty ward and weapon
>
> He helps us clear from every rod
>
> By which we now are smitten.
>
> Still our ancient foe

Girds him to strike a blow.

Might and guile his gear.

His armor striketh fear.

On earth is not his equal.

By our own strength is nothing won.

We court at once disaster.

There fights for us the Champion

Whom God has named our Master.

Would you know his name?

Jesus Christ the same

Lord Sabbath is he.

No other God can be.

The field is his to hold it.

And though the fiends on every hand

Were threatening to devour us,

We would not waver from our stand.

They cannot overpower us.

This world's prince may rave.

However he behave,

He can do no ill.

God's truth abideth still.

One little word shall fell him.

That word they never can dismay.

However much they batter,

For God himself is in the fray

And nothing else can matter.

Then let them take our life,

Goods, honor, children, wife.

We will let all god.

They shall not conquer so,

For God will win the battle.

But for all that, and despite all of Luther's challenges, by translating the whole New Testament into German, he enabled ordinary German folk to read and study Scripture, and to interpret its truths directly— as opposed to merely listening to authoritative sermons delivered by priests. His translations paved the way for the entire Protestant movement, the view that people's relationship to God is direct and need not filter through religious authorities.

Although Luther dwelt in solitude, his bold stand against the church began to catch fire as common men took the lead under his supervision. Luther was in continual conversation with these men: Melanchthon (professor of Greek), Carlstadt (professor at the Castle Church), and Zwilling (a monk trained as Luther had been). They discussed his interpretations, and he helped these men begin to take initiative in leading the people in the reformed faith.

It was during Luther's year away that perhaps the most useful change began to take place within the church. It is recorded by Bainton that "priests married, monks married, and nuns married. Wine in the mass was given to the laity, and priests celebrated the sacrament without vestments in plain clothes. Portions of the mass were recited in the German tongue. Meat was eaten on fast days. Liturgy was a part of their daily religious life." While today, these changes may seem uncontentious, in Luther's time, they represented a radical shift from the Church's traditions. With direct access to scripture, power began shifting to individuals, and those individuals started taking control of their own lives. Luther himself even witnessed the beginning of the movement during his lifetime.

Return from Exile

Luther returned from his exile back to Wittenberg almost a year after he was excommunicated. Though he wasn't "officially" welcomed again, with so much reform already having taken place, it was less likely that he would be arrested. He noticed at once saw just how much chaos ensued from the newfound authority of the individual. Indeed, a day before his return, there was a riot in Wittenberg as students invaded the church and stole a number of books used for mass— all the while using knives and stone to force out priests. Freedom quickly bred liberality and sinful behavior, forcing Luther to weigh in on the relationship between individual freedom and living virtuously.

Carlstadt, one of Luther's leading monks, was influential in helping move the Reformation along moderate lines. One of the most apparent signs of change occurred on Christmas Day, when more than two thousand people met in the Castle Church. A chronicler noted that the whole town gathered to hear a sermon by Carlstadt, who also administered the sacraments. Carlstadt, with the entire city in service, deliberately dressed in a plain black robe as opposed to the garments typically worn by priests. This marked a break from the conventional way in which priests had delivered the sacraments.

Carlstadt challenged the townspeople in their old ways of thinking, saying that there should be no need for fasting and confession before taking the sacraments. He would state as Luther taught, faith alone is needed, also evidenced in a deep heartfelt contrition. As recorded, he said, "See how Christ makes you a sharer in his blessedness if you believe. See how he has cleansed and hallowed you through his promise. Still better, see that Christ stands before you. He takes to form you all of your struggle and doubt, that you may know that through his word you are blessed." Such words echoed Luther's justification of faith.

Moreover, for the first time in their lives, more than two thousand townspeople were able to hear in German, "This is the cup of my blood of the new and eternal testament, spirit and secret of the faith, shed for you to the remission of sins." Then, under Carlstadt's leadership, the town council at Wittenberg issued the first city ordinance of the Reformation: mass would be henceforth be conducted in the same way Carlstadt had demonstrated.

Understanding Luther without talking about people like Carlstadt is impossible. As you read the words of Carlstadt, you read Luther. All the struggles and persecutions that Luther had undertaken were essential to the growth of his followers like Carlstadt. The truths of Scripture began retaking root, and people experienced the reformation of their hearts. Just as Luther had concluded that he no longer had to earn his salvation, so others could hear the gospel truth that

Jesus bore their sins once and for all. In essence, this is the

heart of the great reformation led by Luther and carried forth

by others.

Marriage

Priests practiced celibacy, but Lurther thought this was wrong. For his part, in 1525, about three years after his return from exile, Luther married Katherine von Bora. Luther was forty-two at the time, and Katherine was twenty-six. He wrote, "I believe in marriage, and I intend to get married before I die ... I am not infatuated (with Katherine) though I cherish my wife and I would not exchange Katie for France or for Venice because God has given her to me and other women have worse faults." He then summarized his reasons for marriage, explaining that it was to "please his father, to spite the pope and the Devil, and to seal his witness before martyrdom." We don't find many accounts of Katherine, but one wonders how she might have responded to Luther's reasons for marriage—though perhaps she simply appreciated his boldness and wit.

During his married years, Luther faced different challenges that would change his way of thinking. He wrote that "there is a lot to get used to in the first year of marriage where one wakes up in the morning and finds a pair of pigtails on the pillow which was not there before." His humor and sarcasm never ceased during his years of marriage, as he faced similar tensions as any other couple faces.

After a year of marriage, Katherine bore Luther a son, Hans Luther. Here are Luther's words regarding parenting a baby: "Hans is cutting his teeth and beginning to make a joyous nuisance of himself. These are the joys of marriage of which the pope is not worthy." Even as a parent and husband, he seemingly could never fully separate the Reformation from his gaze. It was so influential in his life that it became a marker for all his experiences.

Luther and Katherine went on to have a total of six children in a span of eight years. One can just imagine the type of distresses and struggles a young Katherine and older Luther faced as first-time parents with so many young ones filling their household.

Luther held conservative views on marriage, as he tried to hold to the tenets of what the Bible stated about the role of men and women in marriage. For Luther, the husband was the head of the wife simply because God created Adam first, and then Eve. All wives were required not only to love their husband but also to honor him in obedience. This idea of ruling over one's wife didn't suggest an exploitative, condescending dominion, but rather leadership with gentleness and love.

Regarding the role of wives, Luther had a characteristically witty way of defining their sphere of influence—he joked that wives had "large hips in order that they could stay at home and sit on them." Childbearing and housekeeping were the limited roles that Luther envisioned for his wife.

One might wonder whether Luther's upbringing, under the strict rule of his parents, influenced the way he parented. For Luther, children were to be ruled by their parents, primarily by the father. He used the metaphor of a magistrate of the state to illuminate how the father should rule over his children, with their obedience required (per the fifth commandment).

On one occasion, it's noted that Luther was so upset that his son was disobedient, he refused to forgive him for three days. Katherine and his Luther's friends eventually had to beg Luther to forgive his son sooner rather than later. When asked why it took so long for Luther to forgive his son, he argued that his son's obedience not only disregarded his father but also offended the great majesty and holiness of God. Interestingly that for someone who took so seriously justification by grace through faith, his parenting at times reflected the attitude of a wrathful judge. One might assume he would have been more gracious to his son since both were forgiven and pardoned by God.

Yet one thing was clear: Luther held God in high esteem for his holiness. Perhaps Luther was never entirely able to separate his experiences of being a monk, trying to achieve perfection with God in complete obedience, from his life after the Reformation began.

Regarding the future marriages of his children, Luther held a view that would impact further generations. Although he didn't hold entirely to arranged marriages, he did believe that marriage should be set within the framework of family relationships. This meant that marriages should be established within families, and while parents should not force their children to marry a specific individual, children also should not resist choices that elders made in their best interest.

Luther viewed marriage and raising a family as one of the most challenging things in his life. He once stated, "Good God, what a lot of trouble there is in marriage. Adam has made a mess of our nature. Think of all the squabbles Adam and Eve must have had in the course of their nine hundred years. Eve would say, 'You ate the apple,' and Adam would retort, 'You gave it to me.'"

Despite his experiences facing physical persecution and death, Luther came to see marriage, not the monastery, as the best school for building character. This view represented a radical shift for Luther, but he found that such virtues as patience, strength, and humility were exercised and strengthened within the family.

Luther said that as husbands had to worry about finances for the rest of their days, so wives had to bear the trials of pregnancy and childbearing. Luther said this about women and childbearing: "You are a woman and your work is pleasing to God. Rejoice in his will. Bring forth the child. Should you die, it is for a noble work and in obedience to God. If you were not a woman, you should wish to be one, that you might suffer and die in so precious and noble a work of God."

Although Luther held the role of the wife in such high regard, he stated that the raising of children was a trial and work for both parents. On several occasions he joked at his children, "Child, what have you done that I should love you so? You have disturbed the whole household with your bawling."

Luther thus held views on marriage and parenting that come in conflict with the prevailing views today. But if anything, the stridency of his views further humanizes Luther. He and

Katherine dealt with troubles any other parents would go through. They had to learn how to balance work, rest, and relationships. Katherine's day was typically spent taking care of the children and animals, in hopes of having time in the evening to talk with her husband. And Luther's day was filled with preaching four times while also lecturing and building relationships with students during meals. They indeed faced difficulty in trying to find time for each other while fulfilling their responsibilities within their respective spheres.

But when everything was said and done, Luther viewed Katherine as his closest neighbor, whom he was bound to love as himself. He fully understood that love was a grace of God throughout the marriage. He said that "the first love is drunken. When the intoxication wears off, then comes the real marriage love." For Luther, love wasn't just filled with pleasantries, but involved an active, intentional effort to "study" one another.

Later writings demonstrate the deep love Luther had for his wife. When Katherine was so sick that he thought she was going to die, he said, "Oh Katie, do not die and leave me." For someone who was so independently focused on accomplishing God's will throughout his life, such an intense and loving attachment to another person was remarkable. On another occasion, when Luther was so sick that he thought he himself was going to die, he said, "My dearest Katie, if it be God's will, accept it. You are mine. You will rest assured of that, and hold to God's word. I did want to write another book on baptism, but God's will be done. May he care for you and Hans." And in Katherine's reply she said, "If it is God's will, I would rather have you with our Lord than here. But I am not thinking just of myself and Hans. There are so many people that need you. But don't worry about us. God will take care of us."

Unlike so many other influential men, who, throughout history, left unfortunate legacies regarding their relationships with their families, Luther was different. The bond he had with his wife was apparently strong and enduring. And, despite his varying personal flaws, Luther's children generally agreed that he was a wonderfully loving father, husband, and human being.

As a father, Luther experienced tragedy as well. When his daughter was only fourteen years old, she became so sick that she was about to die. Luther prayed fervently, "O God, I love her so, but thy will be done." Unfortunately, his daughter passed away in the hands of her father. He reflected, "You will rise and shine like the stars and the sun. How strange it is to know that she is at peace and all is well, and yet to be so sorrowful." Luther was a man of undying faith. Even in his darkest moments, he drew upon God's graces to cast a uplifting light.

Spread of Luther's Teaching

Even as the beginnings of the Reformation made it possible for Luther to return to his hometown, he pursued the much greater goal of spreading the teachings of Scripture across northern Germany. Propaganda that involved tracts and cartoons was the main medium by which this was accomplished. It is said that the sheer number of pamphlets dispersed within just four years exceeded the quantity of any other four-year period of German history. That is to say, Luther and his followers worked doggedly to spread religious reform across Germany and Europe more broadly.

The chief goal of the propaganda was to showcase the abuses of the Roman church, while highlighting the teachings of Christ. In one particular pamphlet, the pope was depicted conversing with Christ:

Christ: "I have no where to lay my head."

Pope: "Sicily is mine. Corsica is mine. Assisi is mine. Perugia is mine."

Christ: "He who believes and is baptized will be saved."

Pope: HE who contributes and receives indulgences will be absolved."

Christ: "Feed my sheep."

Pope: "I shear mine."

Christ: "Put up your sword."

Pope: "Pope Julius killed sixteen hundred in one day."

Propaganda like this simplified for ordinary people the distinction between the Catholic Church's abuses to the fundamental tenets of Scripture.

Another cartoon features a depiction of Luther at his desk, when Satan interrupts with a letter that reads:

We Lucifer, lord of eternal darkness and ruler of all the kingdoms of the world, declare to you, Martin Luther, our wrath and displeasure. We have learned from our legates; the damage you have done in that you have revived the Bible which at our behest has been little used for the last four hundred years. You have persuaded monks and nuns to leave the cloisters in which formerly they served us as well and you are yourself and apostate from our service. Therefore, we will persecute you with burning, drowning and beheading. This is a formal declaration of war, and you will receive no other notices. Sealed with our hellish seal in the City of Damnation on the last day of September 1524.

Cartoons like these further highlighted the abuses of the Church by correlating them with the work of Satan himself. As all effective propaganda creates a stir, so did the pamphlets and cartoons that were dispersed between 1521 and 1524 elicit strong reactions.

It's worth noting that while the purpose of this propaganda was to bring the essential gospel of justification by faith to the hearts and minds of the common folk, Luther featured himself prominently in many of the pamphlets. He was keen on using his own star power. Poet, Hans Sachs referred to him as the "Wittenberg Nightingale," writing this poem:

> Luther teaches that we all
>
> Are involved in Adam's fall.
>
> If man beholds himself within,
>
> He feels the bite and curse of sin.
>
> When dread, despair, and terror seize,
>
> Contrite he falls upon his knees.
>
> Then breaks for him the light of day.
>
> Then the gospel may have sway.

Then sees the Christ of God the Son,

Who for us all things has done.

The law fulfilled, the debt is paid,

Death overcome, the curse allayed,

Hell destroyed, the devil bound,

Grace for us with God has found.

Christ, the Lamb, removes all sin.

By faith alone in Christ we win.

While Luther's teachings were at the forefront, with the goal of furthering their acceptance by all individuals in their various walks of life, he himself was sometimes romanticized.

Other Contributions

Luther developed two catechisms: both the *Large Catechism*, which was intended for adults, and the *Small Catechism*, which was designed for children. Both catechisms were formed from five basic truths: the ten commandments, the Apostle's Creed, baptism, the Lord's Supper and the Lord's Prayer.

Luther wanted to ensure that proper teaching was occurring not only in the church but also in the home. He believed that parents had the responsibility to teach their children in the right way, especially regarding the doctrinal truths of Scripture. Rather than simply placing the authority on the church, Luther created these catechisms with the hopes that they would be used within the home by parents to teach their children. For example, he even instructed that parents should use memorization of the catechism as a means of motivation for children before they could eat their meal—and if children were unwilling to learn the catechism before eating, then they simply would not eat that meal.

Besides the catechisms, Luther also developed liturgy for public worship. Luther may not have considered himself very skilled in music, but he played the lute and sang. It is noted that he also composed at least ten hymns, and he produced simple melodies and harmonic arrangements within the hymns. More than music, it was the content of his lyrics that inspired. Regarding music, he wrote:

> Music is a fair and lovely gift of God which has often wakened and moved me to the joy of preaching...Experience proves that next to the Word of God, only music deserves to be extolled as the mistress and governess of the feelings of the human heart. My heart bubbles up and overflows in response to music, which has so often refreshed me and delivered me from dire plagues.

In 1524, Luther compiled a book of twenty-three hymns that he wrote and helped compose. One of his most notable hymns was from his reflection on Psalm 130, "In Direst Need":

> I cry to thee in direst need.
>
> O God, I beg thee hear me.
>
> To my distress I pray give heed.
>
> O Father, draw thou ear me.
>
> If thou shouldst wish to look upon
>
> The wrong and wickedness I've done,
>
> How could I stand before thee?

> With thee is naught but untold grace
>
> Evermore forgiving.
>
> We cannot stand before thy face,
>
> Not by the best of living.
>
> No man boasting may draw near.
>
> All the living stand in fear.

Thy grace alone can save them.

Therefore in God I place my trust,

My own claim denying.

Believe in him alone I must,

On his sole grace relying.

He pledged to me his plighted word.

My comfort is in what I heard.

There will I hold forever.

In these lines, one can observe the very struggles and distresses Luther experienced during the early parts of his life, as he was subjected to impending death. But within his distress, one can also see the very source of strength Luther found in God, in whom he believed through both the joys and trials of life.

Luther the Preacher

With the continued establishment of the Reformation, Luther evidently assisted the rest of the clergy to make sure that the Scriptures were explicitly taught. Whereas prior to the Reformation, the altar seemed to take precedence over the pulpit, Luther reinforced the importance of preaching. He believed that salvation was found through the Word and that the Word was the place for healing all of life's struggles.

Luther, alongside others, took part in a campaign in which there were three services on Sunday. Each service had a different theme, whether a teaching on the Epistles, the Gospels, or the catechism. During the week, the church was always opened, and each day a minister delivered a sermon.

It is known that Luther was a message-preaching workhorse. Not only did he give family devotions at home, but he often spoke multiple times on Sundays, and during the week as well. In his career post-excommunication, he gave over 2,300 sermons. And in one particular year, Luther delivered 195 sermons in just 145 days.

What drove Luther to maintain his role as a preacher throughout the years? He was convinced that the role of the minister was to study the Word and deliver it faithfully to members. Moreover, he constantly reminded himself of the diligence of apostles such as Peter and Paul. In a letter Luther wrote to a discouraged minister, he contended:

> If Peter and Paul were here, they would scold you because you wish right off to be as accomplished as they. Crawling is something, even if one is unable to walk. Do your best. If you cannot preach an hour, then preach half an hour or a quarter of an hour. Do not try to imitate other people. Center on the shortest and simplest points, which are the very heart of the matter, and leave the rest to God. Look solely to his honor and

not to applause. Pray that God will give you a mouth and to your audience ears. I can tell you preaching is not a work of man. Although I am old and experienced, I am afraid every time I have to preach. You will most certainly find out three things: first, you will have prepared your sermon as diligently as you know how, and it will slip through your fingers like water; second, you may abandon your outline and God will give you grace. You will preach your very best. The audience will be pleased, but you won't. And thirdly, when you have been unable in advance to pull anything together, you will preach acceptably both to your hearers and to yourself. So pray to God and leave all the rest to him.

We thereby get insight of the type of drive, determination, and persistence that Luther carried through his years of preaching. It is likely that these words to a tired minister were the very words that helped keep Luther himself steady amidst the task of delivering sermons day in and day out.

What kind of preacher was Luther? It was clear that Luther delivered messages by explaining the text while interweaving his personal experiences. He was not a cut and dried preacher, because of how he applied the text to one's personal life.

Above all, Luther adamantly maintained that a life of prayer undergirded the preparation of a sermon. He is famously known to have said, "I have so much to do today that I shall the next three hours in prayer." Yet for Luther, the issue wasn't the length of time he spent in prayer, but rather the focus of his whole body on prayer.

There is a story of Martin Luther's barber, who asked for advice on prayer. Luther's response included an open letter called "A Simple Way to Pray." He wrote, "What else is it but tempting God when your mouth babbles and the mind wanders to other thoughts?" He used a metaphor that the barber would understand to further explain his point:

> So, a good and attentive barber keeps his thoughts, attention, and eyes on the razor and hair and does not forget how far he has gotten with his shaving or cutting. If he wants to engage in too much conversation or let his mind wander or look somewhere else he is likely to cut his customer's mouth, nose, or even his throat. Thus, if anything is to be done well, it requires the full attention of all one's senses and members, as the proverb says, 'He who thinks of many things, thinks of nothing and does nothing right.' How much more does prayer call for concentration and singleness of heart if it is to be a good prayer!

In the letter, he also described his daily routine of praying to the Lord. He wrote:

> First, when I feel that I have become cool and joyless in prayer because of other tasks or thoughts (for the flesh and the devil always impede and obstruct prayer), I take my little psalter, hurry to my room, or, if it be the day and hour for it, to the church where a congregation is assembled and, as time permits, I say quietly to myself and word-for-word the Ten Commandments, the Creed, and, if I have time, some words of Christ or of Paul, or some psalms, just as a child might do. It is a good thing to let prayer be the first business of the morning and the last at night.

If anything could be said of Luther and prayer, it was that in every corner of his life, whether in trouble or triumph, Luther was quick to honor God by offering up his supplications,

112

requests, and thanksgiving. Perhaps, if anything made Luther the man he was, it was his constant drive to experience the presence of God. The key to understanding Luther, then, isn't Luther himself, but God, who transformed him and gave him the strength to achieve great things.

Who Was Martin Luther?

Luther died on February 18, 1546, at the age of sixty-two, after he traveled back to his birth city of Eisleben, Germany. The journey took such a toll on the sixty-two-year-old Luther that he became terminally ill. He spent his very last hours on earth in the place of his birth, conscious enough to confess his sins while affirming his faith in Christ alone. Then he died, accompanied by one of his closest disciples.

The last sermon Luther preached came from two texts: Psalm 68:19 and John 3:16. It is no coincidence that his final message centered on the very truth of the gospel.

How can one summarize Luther and his impact? It must be from the lens of faith and religion. Luther's high view of the Bible, coupled with a radical persistence to stand up to Scriptural truths against hypocrisy, would be the mark that he impressed most firmly upon generations to come. He wrote,

"The true Christian pilgrimage is not to Rome, but to the prophets, the Psalms, and the Gospels."

This is where Luther laid his life—within the very pages of the Old and New Testaments. It was in the book of Romans that Luther's life was forever transformed, where he placed his faith in Jesus for the forgiveness of sins. It was there in the Gospels that He came to understand how the life and death of Christ were the sole appeasement of God's wrath of judgment on him. It was there, within the core of grace and power, that Luther could stand against the authority of the Church despite the fear of persecution and death.

Made in the USA
Columbia, SC
04 November 2019